Investing in the Stock Market for Broke Folks!

A Simple Guide for Penny Pinchers

Delia Williams

Copyright: 2019 Delia Williams All rights reserved.

ISBN: 9781731003874

Published by Delia Williams www.dtinvestmentglobal.com

Edited by Delisa Rodgers-Fields

Cover design: Delia Williams Printed in the United States of America

All rights reserved under International Copyright Law: Contents and/or cover may not be reproduced in whole or in part in any form without the express written consent of the publisher.

Disclaimer:

The information contained within is offered as general advice from the author which has not been tailored for your personal situation. The author is not liable for any financial loss because of investments-based content that has been taken directly or indirectly from this book. Investment products are not FDIC insured. Investing involves substantial risk.

Dedication:

This book is dedicated to Mom and Dad.

Table of Contents

Introduction: 7

Let's Start With the Basis 10

Hard Truth 15

Understand The Game 19

Small Minds Do Think Alike: 27

Lottery time: 34

Take the limits off: 42

Payday: 48

Introduction:

If you are broke, then this the right book for you. It is funny in a way how a person who does not have enough money to pay their own bills takes an interest in investing in the stock market. I believe you are like me in that regard. You are sick and tired of being sick and tired. Being broke is not fun at all. If you are one paycheck from being broke, I am talking to you as well. So, what do you do when you want to invest in the stock market, but you are broke?

Opportunities in life will come and go. What are you going to do with your opportunity to invest in the stock market? This book is an essential book for broke folks. I have yet to use any algebraic concepts at school. This is a necessary book for everyday people who are broke.

I do not have time to sell a dream implying that investing in the stock market is going to be a 1, 2, 3 Solution. Nor do I have time to convince you that by purchasing this book, all your problems will be solved. My number one focus on writing this book is to introduce you to Investor Broke Jones who represents broke people around the world who are interested in generating wealth.

Investor Broke Jones has lived the "good life" and as a result, has accumulated tremendous debt, has a low credit rating and has no savings or retirement plans. Investor Broke Jones is you and I who have lived careless lifestyles being irresponsible with our finances. So, throughout this book, I will introduce Investor Broke Jones as a simple example. I believe you should create a plan, work diligently to pay off debt, and create your wealth portfolio. It does not take much money to invest in the stock market. Investing in the stock market represents one part of your wealth portfolio. To live a comfortable lifestyle, you will need to do more than work and earn an income.

The steps to success are darn simple in this book. It is not my intention to confuse you in by including fancy stock market terms or steps. There were hundreds of Americans who were victims of the fancy talker and Ponzi schemer, Bernie Madoff. You do not need a prestigious degree or be a licensed stockbroker to invest in the stock market. Investing is possible for average folks like you and me. We can live a financially free lifestyle and pass on our knowledge to the next generation.

To create wealth, you will need to generate a portfolio that includes stocks, businesses, and real estate. If you can create a can-do attitude and mindset, establish goals, training/education, and an investment strategy, you should we well on your way to long-term returns. My goal is to provide simple steps for working people around the world.

During 2000 and 2008, there were two major market crashes. These market crashes left investors in a state of shock. Investors did not know what to do or whom they should trust. Being broke from not receiving enough of income is one thing. Many investors placed their trust in a financial broker named, Bernie Madoff. Mr. Madoff swindled his way in the lives of many Americans and took off with their retirement and life savings. He took advantage of people with a lack of financial knowledge. Do you really need a Bernie Madoff in your life? It is easy to get caught up with the hype, ranting, and raving in the news. As a smart investor, learn when it is time to turn off your television.

To be successful when investing in the stock market start by reading books, listening to podcasts, and receiving hands-on investing training to ensure your confidence and knowledge before you start. Another tip to be successful as an investor is to understand the company's financial reports and rules in the stock market when you are buying or selling. A broke person should be looking for opportunities to make additional income. I will discuss ways the stock market can help you in a later chapter. By using the stock market as an opportunity to earn additional income, you can live a life on your own terms.

Let's Start With the Basis

As a child, I was taught to graduate high school, college, and go to work or serve in the military. I understand now that the middle to poor class speaks the same financial language. A person can be poor regarding how they view obtaining wealth. The 1% make rules for the 99%. The rich speak a different language. The problem here is you work so hard to become the very thing you are trying to avoid. There are thousands to millions of individuals around the world with a similar mindset who have embraced the concept of going to college, getting a job, and retiring in your 60's with a retirement plan. The difference here is the individual's mindset about obtaining wealth.

Regardless of your personal situation, obtaining financial knowledge is your key to living your life on the beach. You should know that avoidance and being held accountable is not the answer. There is only a matter of time before the very thing you avoid will slap you in the face and say to you, "Hello, here I am!" The middle, working, and poor classes speak the same language by enforcing college, getting a job, and retiring with a company manufacture retirement plan. This class represents most of the population.

Further, there is still not enough emphasis placed on being an employer instead of the employee. Being the employer increases your financial net worth. Working as an employee sets your pay, sets your insurance and retirement, and offers the potential of a yearly raise. I lived in the poor, working, middle class. I wondered how the rich stayed rich and the poor stayed poor. One way the poor remains poor is a misunderstanding of how to generate wealth.

Many individuals in the poor class are consumers instead of the investor. I lived most of my life as a consumer. I focused on liabilities rather than assets. I was the girl with the name brand items and started introducing my daughter to the same concepts. I quickly dismantled my views about finances and generating wealth. I noticed how the rich earn money in their sleep. I do not know about you, but I always wanted to know how they were able to make money in their sleep.

Consider McDonald's, Corporation. McDonald's has a real estate empire. I find their business structure to be an amazing one. On the forefront, consumers will see McDonald's restaurants throughout the world. On the backend, McDonald's has established thousands of real estate businesses. This is structured to offset the restaurant's expenses resulting in fewer taxes than the average working, middle-class family. The rich stay rich by paying less in taxes. I believe the rich stay rich by staying away from get-rich-quick schemes. There are no right or wrong answers to developing wealth; however, there is a right answer for how to keep it.

The difference between the rich and the poor's understanding of wealth, building multiple streams of income, and paying less in taxes is that the rich tend to have assets (real estate) that offset their taxes. This is one of the reasons why a corporation like McDonald's can pay fewer taxes than a person in a lower-class bracket. The tax laws are fair and legal. You just need the right tax accountant to assist you. Just think about whom the tax laws were written to protect. Individuals in the middle class should study them more closely. A person's taxes can become excessive monthly and yearly liability.

I did not learn the concept of generating wealth until a few years ago. Moreover, guess what? I am still learning. I had to face the very thing I had been avoiding which was being a horrible financial manager over my money. I did not pay my bills on time. I did not save my money; I chose to instead party. I even purchased personal items and treated myself to salon visits, manicures, and pedicures rather than pay my bills. I went vacationing with borrowed money and didn't realize how my financial health was being jeopardized until I reached adulthood. If you were anything like me, this is your chance to be on the road to financial freedom.

Please understand being on the road to financial freedom will come with challenges. Here are steps to assist you in becoming a successful investor:

1. Being committed
2. Pursuing education
3. Setting goals
4. Having patience
5. Developing an investment strategy
6. Understanding your risk tolerance
7. Minding your emotions
8. Setting realistic expectations
9. Paying due diligence
10. Reevaluating your strategy or plan

I believe a significant problem people are faced with is how to invest in the stock market without money. The answer is simple. You will need to eliminate debt and begin with what you have. I have overheard financial advisors offering suggestions to beginner investors about getting starting in the stock market based upon investing a certain amount of money. I cannot imagine how disconcerting those requirements may appear for those sincerely hoping to start investing and generating wealth. There are countless people whom I have conversated with who do not know where to start. Sadly, many do not believe they have enough money to begin investing. If that person is you, I believe you should start with what you have.

Now let us talk about real life - you know bills, having little to no income to invest, and misunderstanding the entire process. First, you should take into consideration your debt to monthly expense ratio. Create a monthly expense report. In this report, include your income and liabilities. Be sure to include all of your expenses. A personal budget will include primary and secondary incomes. The second section will include monthly expenses such as your home, vehicle, food, utilities, and other (credit cards, gifts, vacation, charity, etc.). Make sure to tally both your income and expenses.

The third section will include a summary of your total income and total expenses. The total income is deducted from the expenses. Once your budget is completed, create a plan to pay off your debts. You may choose to make payments on your debt until they have a zero balance. You may also choose to tackle your higher interest debt, pay them off, and then proceed to clear the balance on lower debt. It is my philosophy to create a debt repayment plan that works for your family. After completing this report, you will discover how mounting debt can interfere with your ability to invest in the stock market. How much would you have to invest if you did not have a credit card or a car loan? Try not to become overwhelmed after completing this exercise. Remain persistent and focused on your goals. It will all work out in the end.

Years ago, I accumulated mountains of debt, and as a result, my unpaid bills were turned over to collection agencies. Since I did not educate myself about credit, debt, or investing, I decided not to pay these bills. Unfortunately, as a young woman, I did not perceive how unpaid bills and adverse credit reporting would affect me later on in life. It was not until much later that it occurred to me how being careless with my money as a young woman would impact future financial decisions. My mistakes would soon play an essential role in any financial decision that I made. Consequently, I decided to get my act together and confront my financial situation.

At first, I felt so overwhelmed and defeated. I did not know what to do. It was not until I created a positive mindset, developed an "I can do it attitude," that I realized it was possible for me to rediscover financial well-being. It feels amazing to tell people that if a single mother of three can do it, you can as well. It is a sad fact that many families are one paycheck away from being broke. Keep in mind that being broke does not necessarily refer to your income bracket. Being broke can represent a person who is one paycheck away from losing everything. There are individuals in the lower, working, middle, and upper-class brackets who are broke. You may wonder how a person living in the upper-income class bracket is broke. This answer is simple. Many middle- and upper-class citizens do not have an emergency fund, retirement, or any other type of investments. They are living paycheck to paycheck. You can be a part of the working class with little to no debt and be able to invest in the stock market. On the other hand, your dream home may come with a hefty price tag and can be considered as an asset. If a house produces income for you, it is considered as an asset. A car, on the other hand, is an example of a liability.

Hard Truth

Most people were taught to graduate from college and start a family. Needless to say, some did not realize the cost of attending college and starting a family. Most families are still paying college-related fees into their late adulthood as well as managing expenses related to raising a family. If you do not have any money left over from your paycheck after paying your monthly expenses, reconsider how you are spending your money.

When you think about investing in the stock market, you may feel as if you need a lot of money start out. Nothing can be further from the truth. I suggest that you begin trading in the stock market with what you have. There are success stories of countless individuals and families that disciplined themselves while working a full-time job and have retired as millionaires. I believe the first step to investing with little to no money is finding a solution to earn more money.

The hard truth here is that something in your life will need to change. How often do you dine out? How often do you shop? Is your current car loan affordable? There are numerous people who party their funds away at the local bars and clubs every weekend. If that is you, how much you do spend on average at the bar or club? Think of this: how much will you save if you manage to cut unnecessary expenses in half or eliminate them totally? Let us use shopping and going to the bar as your expenses.

People are faced with car notes, mortgage loans, student loans, or credit card debts. What makes it difficult to invest in stocks while in debt is the money that can be used to purchase stocks are being used to make payments on a loan. A great way to eliminate debt is to start paying high-interest debt down first. Once you realize which bill has the highest interest rate, start with that bill. Some interest rates on loans or credit cards are as high as 18% or more. Entertainment expenses can be costly as well.

For example, if you are on an outing that costs $150.00 twice a week, it totals $300.00 a month. At the end of the year, the total of those expenses average $3,600.00. Over a period of ten years of spending $3,6000, you've spent $36,000. This may not be the case for you. There are several stocks you can invest in with $3,600. The Coca Cola company is a stock that is traded on the New York Stock Exchange (NYSE). The ticker symbol is KO and is displayed as such on the Big Board or the NYSE. As of December 2018, KO's price per share averaged $46.00. Using the $3,600 from shopping and going to the bar, you can purchase around 77 shares of stock each year. Within ten years, you could have accumulated 770 shares in the Coca Cola Company.

Debt can become a big deal and a massive hindrance for investing in the stock market. Methods you can use to save so you can invest in the stock market are:

1. Open a saving account

2. Open a money market account

3. Stash money under your mattress. You may have heard stories of people saving their money under a mattress, but this is not the way I recommend saving money. Take a moment to smile because everything will be okay. I am just kidding. Opening a certificate of deposit is another option.

A certificate of deposit (CD) is another safe option. A CD requires a set amount of money to open the account that must be kept in the account for a certain period of time. At the maturity date, you will have access to what you have saved in the CD. Be sure to shop around for the best rates, minimum deposit, and terms. Money from any of these accounts can be used to fund your brokerage account. Although opening a savings account produces low-interest rates, it is another safe way to save your money. A money market account is an option and available through your bank.

Money from a money market account tends to incur higher interest rates. Take time to verify rates, terms and conditions, and the withdrawal process. The challenges are changing a negative financial mindset by creating a financial plan. Have you examined your current financial situation? If not, why? It is essential to examine your financial situation to come up with solutions. One financial solution is to write down all your bills. After you have created a list of expenses, start by placing the company's name, interest rate, and the minimum and total amount payment due. Be honest with yourself. The next step is to earn additional income.

Do you have a hobby? My 15-year-old daughter loves to sew. She loves to create pillows, blankets, scarfs, and sachets. She has a desire to make gowns and dresses in the future. My daughter's talents are now an income producing talent. You have a special talent that can produce extra money for your household as well. Can you sing?

A prime example is this: there is a company in America that hires singers to sing songs to customers in uncommon places. Let's say your sister's birthday is next week. You can hire this company to have an individual sing your sister happy birthday at her job, bowling alley, hair salon, etc. There are tons of ways to produce extra income. You will have to stick to what you are good at and create a business to generate income.

If you are in debt, have your interest paid off by paying the minimum balance on your accounts. If you use these concepts, you will be able to pay all your debts promptly. You can be just like many individuals around me who do not follow my directions. In that case, you will still be able to retire with saving your money in a local bank with an interest rate of 0.1. Investing and patience are the keys. The concept of generating wealth can be simple or hard depending on if you can follow instructions. To generate wealth, you will need to develop positive financial habits, spend your time wisely on things that really matter, find a mentor, and create a wealth portfolio.

Understand The Game

There are four assets classes to generate wealth which are: businesses, paper (stocks/bonds), real estate, and commodities. Creating wealth will take time. You cannot create wealth by having a magic solution; however, you can achieve it with what you have. How has partying helped you generate wealth? If you take a few minutes and analyze those behaviors, you will find that you are wasting your money. How much money have you wasted this year? The money you wasted this year could have been used to create your wealth portfolio. Think of creating wealth as a full pie that is cut into slices. We will build a wealth portfolio by focusing on one slice of the pie at a time.

In this book, we will focus on the slice of the pie that represents the stock market. Now, you will need to cut your stock market investment slice into several small pieces. These pieces will represent types of investment securities. For example, if cut your slice into five small pieces, each piece can represent different investment securities. For example, a piece can be shares of stocks, bonds, index funds, mutual funds, or cryptocurrency. Another example of that slice is divided into several pieces called exchange-traded funds (ETF's), commodities, stocks, mutual funds, and bonds. Other types of investment products are real estate investment trusts (REITs), annuities, certificates of deposit (CD's), or money market funds. Your portfolio will be unique to fit into your personal situation. My investment style will not be like yours and vice versa.

As a future investor, you will need to set a goal. All investors will learn how to generate wealth differently. Generating wealth can occur by developing a service or a product for consumers to purchase. There are so many wonderful products in the world. Think about this product for a moment. How many people wrap blankets around them while sitting on the couch watching television? The Snuggie is a product for children and adults.

Individuals can wrap themselves in a Snuggie which is a cozy blanket in the comfort of their own home. This product was and still is a brilliant way to capitalize on something you are already doing to generate income. After your production and business expense has been paid, you can invest, save, put more back into your business, and pay yourself. You see, there is no right or wrong way to generate income. You will need to generate some type of income to invest in the stock market. After you have the income, the goal is to start.

Your goals should be specific. How are going to reach your financial goals? First, take a few moments to name your list. For example, if you would like to get out of debt, your list can be named the Financial Freedom Plan or Retirement List. I have several lists. You can have a list like mine. Just name your list, Invest Like a Boss, and make sure you send me an email or tag me on social media. Each item on your list will require a goal and timeframe to complete it. Only focus on a few goals at a time. If you have 15 goals, try to focus on the top 5 at a time until you complete all of them. After you complete the five goals, move on to the next 5.

I believe it is sad to dream about a particular lifestyle and never obtain it. Completing your goals will take time, and that is all right. It is time to dream again. I know dreaming can be childish, in a sense. You can live the lifestyle of your dreams without being in financial bondage, but you are going to work for it. The truth here is reality and life challenges. For some of us, reality came at an early age. Reality and life challenges knocked some of us off our feet. Don't allow reality to rob you from living your best life. Your reality is everyday experiences which include learning the foundation principles of money and generating wealth.

My reality came knocking on my door after having a bucket full of debt and bad credit. I did not understand the principles of money. Investing in the stock market and generating wealth was not taught in our school systems. We are taught Algebra or Trigonometry as if we will use them in a real-life situation. Now tell me, how can you use Algebra to generate wealth? Is it possible to invest in real estate by using Trigonometry? The answer to this is, No!

As an investor, setting goals are essential. Your financial goals should not be vague such as, "I want to invest in the stock market." Okay, so does everyone else. An example of a clear goal is, "I would like to invest in the stock market to cover the startup costs when I open my mall business. The startup cost is $15,000." With a clear and measurable goal in sight, you can then select the right investments to help you meet that goal.

Are you able to measure your goal? Investing in the stock market and creating goals go hand to hand. Let's say you would like to take a vacation or save for a down payment on a home. Do you realize each item listed above requires goals to be established? Maybe you are like me, investing to leave a financial legacy for your children and create multiple income streams. What are you investing to achieve? After you determine what you are investing for, you will need to create a timeframe for your goals. Make sure you have short-term, mid-term, and long-term investing goals. Take a few moments and create a list for your goals.

Now that you have a timeframe, list how much money will each item cost you. If you are investing to generate income for retirement, how much do you need? You may want to invest in the stock market to start a new business, how much will that cost you? You can also invest in the stock market to fund a dream vacation. Let's say your dream vacation to Iceland will could cost $7,000. You will need to create a budget to meet each investment goal.

An investor can choose from hundreds to thousands of investment securities such as stocks, bonds, exchange-traded funds (ETF's), mutual funds, index funds, or other investments. The primary goal here is to build wealth through investments. Selecting the right investment security is essential. Researching investments, diversification, and sticking to your plan is an option for investors to follow. You do not need an investment broker to invest in the stock market, nor do you need to become a genius to invest.

If you invest in the stock market and receive a return on 8%, that will be great. You can also invest in the stock market to receive a higher return on your money. An investor can lose all their money as well. Investing does come with its fair share of risks. There is no guarantee you will make money from investing in the stock market. Without risk, there is no reward. What you do have to lose when you are already at the bottom? The only option you have is to level up. It is time to rise and put your foot to the pavement and invest like a boss. I do not know about you, but I am tired of receiving a 0.01% interest at the bank.

There are many options available for broke folks to invest in the stock market. If you still have a 9-5 job, have you considered starting a business? I know you are thinking, "How can I start a business if I am broke?" This answer is simple. Let's say you are a Math or an English teacher. You can launch a tutoring service. Start off meeting students in the library or a coffee shop. After you have successfully operated your service for a few months or years, expand your business. Yes, I do understand there is more to starting a business than meeting at the library. I am only providing an example with which to use your talent(s) to general additional money.

Creating multiple streams of income is an excellent option for broke folks to invest.

Before you start, make sure your first source of income is secure. I believe your first step is to increase your knowledge about starting a business so you can invest in the future. In life, we pay others for skills and knowledge we do not have. Take into consideration the average doctor's visit or fees from a lawyer. A person can increase their knowledge base by reading, enrolling in a course, or socializing with colleagues, friends, and professionals.

Being broke is frustrating and no fun at all. Trying to get out of debt will take much work. If you are willing to work, you will achieve your financial goals. It is okay to start planning ways to generate income. The average millionaire has seven streams of income. Make sure you focus on one income stream at a time. After you master that one, you can move on to another stream of income. One stream of income is earned income which comes from your current job. If you continue in your comfort zone, you will continue to experience the same results. Profit income is when you sell a product or service like the Snuggie example I provided in the previous chapter.

Rental income is another stream of income. Housing (real estate) is an asset. It is the type of money earned in your sleep. Another source of income is royalty income. This money derives from items that have copyrights, patents, or franchises. Just imagine how much the owner of McDonald's is making from individuals purchasing franchise licenses from them around the world. Interest income is money you receive from banks or bonds.

Being a broke investor, you may want to consider dividend income. This type of income derives from purchasing dividend-paying stocks. A person can receive dividend income from stocks when they become a shareholder in the company. Capital gain is another stream of income you can receive. Investors receive capital gain income when they sell their investment. An investor can receive dividend and interest income from investing in the stock market. Be aware of a few stock market terms and concepts as you embark upon this journey. The stock market is a place where investment securities are sold and purchased.

The United States has two well-known stock markets which are the NASDAQ and the New York Stock Exchange (NYSE). The NASDAQ is an online stock market. The NYSE has a trading floor. Both stock market exchanges have thousands to millions of investment securities that are sold and purchased such as stocks, bonds, exchange-traded funds (ETF's), index funds, commodities, etc. They are sold and purchased when the markets are open.

Write an investment strategy. There is no great small plan or bad big plan. Your goal is to focus on a plan. So, let's say you want to invest in bonds which are like I.O. U's. A bond is a debt security. There are several types of bonds such as municipal, treasury, corporate, or government. I believe your portfolio should be well diversified among several asset classes. A portfolio is a pool of investments. For example, Investor Broke Jones can have a portfolio that includes bonds, stocks, cryptocurrency, and exchange-traded funds (ETF's). Your portfolio will be unique to fit your personal financial needs.

Investor Broke Jones understand the principles of gaining wealth. Investor Broke Jones decided to focus on investing in the stock market first; therefore, Investor Broke Jones' portfolio can have different types of bonds, stocks, mutual funds, and index funds. The terms on how Investor Broke Jones invests his money will depend on his investment style. Investor Broke Jones is an aggressive investor. His stock market portfolio may consist of 75% stocks, 20% bonds, and 5% cash. Throughout, Investor Broke Jones' portfolio will change as he meets his investment goals.

When Investor Broke Jones started to invest, he was an aggressive investor because he partied a lot and now is a late investor. As Broke Jones continued to invest in the stock market, he decided to be a moderate investor until retirement. Your risk level may change as your investment goals are met. The average saving account may yield an annual interest rate of 2%, if you are lucky. Have you noticed the lower and middle-class focus more on saving their money rather than investing it? We spend so much time wasting time and forfeiting a return on our investment.

I have several degrees, and none of them taught me how to generate wealth. Reflecting on my decision to attend college was solely based upon the norm and what a person was supposed to do in society. My high school days were not a walk in the park. I was uninterested in finances, literacy, or school. I was just ready to be done with school and had no plans for the future. I was confused. During my high school years, I was a B to a C average student. Even though I was a B-C, student I always knew I want to be a boss. Walt Disney and Henry Ford were individuals who did not finish college. Both individuals achieved great wealth and success that have played an essential influence in the family entertainment business and the automobile industry. Attending college is not a prerequisite to acquiring wealth.

I heard a saying that A students usually work for the C students. Do you believe this phrase? Whether this is true or not, you should know that working hard, learning, and endurance so that you can generate wealth is not for everyone. My personality, willingness to learn and working skills molded me into the person I am today. I did not use anything I learn from my master's degree to achieve this. I knew I was a leader from childhood. I was the status quo challenger, just confused about the process of becoming an entrepreneur. I did not know anyone who was an entrepreneur when I was a child.

Please don't get me wrong; I am not against college education. Certain universities are unaffordable to the working, middle-class family. Education is the key; however, after you have received a college education, a person can potentially pay the tuition balance off closer towards retirement. Now you cannot tell me this is absurd. It funny in a sense how much society places emphasis on education rather than financial freedom. To make things worse, we land a job after we complete school that in many cases, has nothing to do with our degree. I will be the first person to tell you this entire process needs to stop these systems. Generating wealth will come with failures; however, it is important not to fall and stay down or be afraid of money.

Small Minds Do Think Alike:

Sometimes, I feel as if it was a setup from birth. I remember being excited about my first job. I was hired at the tender age of 16 years old. After working for almost three weeks, I received my first paycheck. Oh boy, I was elated. I remember cashing my checks at check cashing centers or the local store. I had no clue about bank accounts and forget about saving money. During that timeframe, I did not properly learn how to save money. Believe it or not, there were limited people who had bank accounts who were connected to me.

Do you see how the lack of financial knowledge can limit one early in life? I did not know anyone who taught about developing positive financial habits. After I cashed my checks, I spent all my money. I was a teenager living the flashy lifestyle. I did not avoid spending because I had no responsibilities besides going to high school and working. Those same negative financial habits rolled over into my adulthood. When I finally learned about the secrets to success and wealth, it was already too late. That was what I had to accept about my lack of financial knowledge.

It was not my mother or father's fault. The provided me with information that was instilled in them, and I am very grateful for each lesson learned. Now think about this for a moment. How rich is your inner circle? Do you have individuals in your inner circle who are teaching you how to generate wealth? Nowadays people like to party, party, and party some more. After you finish partying, the same problem will be looking at you in the face. Birds of a feather indeed flock together. Have you ever been around a person and you questioned the way you felt or thought about money?

Being a bad manager over my own finances allowed me to accumulate a mountain of debt. I had a mess to clean which took me years to accomplish but guess what? The same individuals I was partying with could not assist me in generating wealth. Had I known more about financial investments, I would have started at the age of 16 years old. The earlier you start investing in the stock market, the better it will be. My job offered a retirement, but I could not imagine engaging in manual labor for the rest of my life. There was a sweet woman who gracefully worked that job until she retired. I believe she was in her 70's. Do you want to work until age 70?

As an employee, participating in your company's retirement plan is a way to invest. An example of employee sponsored plans is Thrift Savings Plan (TSP), 401k, or 403(b). This is an easy and automatic way to invest. You can start planning for your retirement at the age of 18. Just think about if you saved at around $25.00 a month. I noticed individuals who only invest in their company's retirement account at times think the same way.

I used to think the same way until I learned the simple concepts of how to generate wealth and that is what I want to teach you. The full retirement age is 67; however, if a person is 62 years old, they can receive a reduced amount of their retirement benefits. I do not know about you but, I plan on spending time on a beach front property with my toes in the sand before the age of 67. The retirement age 67 is for individuals who were born after 1960.

Financial illiteracy is one of the reasons why I am writing this book. It is imperative for lower, working, and middle-class families to learn how to generate wealth. How are you going to spend time with your loved ones if you are unable to retire? It breaks my heart when I see an individual beyond their retirement age who are still working. I have noticed these make up certain types of people. The first types are early investors.

These are individuals who invested in their company's retirement plan and have other assets to generate wealth. The second types are the 'take what I can receive' investors. These investors accept the terms and conditions to their company's retirement plan. Many times, these individuals will retire with benefits at their retirement age. The third types are the late Boomers. These investors knew retirement was knocking on their door but were unable to invest in their company's 401k retirement plan during a specific timeframe in their life. At the appropriate time, the late boomers can invest a certain portion of their check into their retirement plan.

The last type is the procrastinator. These individuals have no desire to invest in their company's retirement plan. In some cases, the procrastinator delays everything, including the fact that he or she will retire one day. The procrastinator is typically working after their retirement age.

The sad truth is this, we all must face retirement age. It is essential to understand that your social security benefit can increase or decrease according to the age you retire. If you decide to retire before your retirement age, your benefit may decrease. Retiring at the appropriate age could guarantee you receive the full benefit amount. Are you ready to retire? Financial decisions you make now will have an impact on your future. Being retirement ready is starting out with a plan. It is also good to consider your Medicare or Medicaid plans and insurance. Some things to consider are contributing to a 401(k) plan, Traditional IRA, or Roth IRA.

A 401(k) plan is a company-sponsored retirement plan. In the past, companies offered pension funds. A person received their pension funds during their retirement; however, companies have done away with pension funds and have implemented 401(k) plans back in the 1980's. I believe the companies became smarter and deceived the average Joe's like you and me. The goal of the 401(k) plan is to have the employee take control of what they invest in. In most cases, employee sponsored plan includes mutual funds, bonds, stocks, etc. Therefore, if you do not contribute to your 401(k) plan, then you will have not any money in it.

Unless your company is contributing or matching a certain amount of funds into your company's 401(k), there are penalties and taxes if you elect to take your contribution before retirement age. Now, do you see why I stated earlier that companies are becoming smarter because the cost of pension was too expensive? If a person died who was receiving a pension, their spouse was eligible to receive those benefits. It was only a matter of time until your employer served the ball back into your court. Pension funds were created for working and middle-class individuals.

A Traditional IRA plan is a way to plan for your retirement as well. As of 2018, the Traditional IRA's annual contribution's limit was $5,500 if you are under 50 years old and for ages 50 and up, you can contribute up to $6,500 per year. A traditional IRA is another way to grow your money for retirement. A person can select investments for their IRA.

Another way to invest for your retirement is Roth IRA. A Roth IRA contribution limits are $5,500 for people under 50 years old, and if you are over 50 years old, you are eligible for contributions up to $6,50. Check out your company's investment firm or another to open an IRA account. Make sure you learn more about them to select the right one for your situation.

Do you understand why it is important to be around like-minded people? Small minds will think a lot because they tend to repeat cycles from generation to generation. Most of us were told to enroll in college and work a 9-5 until retirement. News flash! This does not have to be your story. As I mentioned before, there are several ways for broke folks to invest. One way is if you decide to contribute to your company's 401(k) plan. Two other options are Traditional or Roth IRA's.

Make a note for yourself to remind you of the contribution amount. Yes, it is right there are limited contributions to IRA's; however, this does not mean you have to contribute that amount. It is essential to start with what you have. If you only have $20, make sure you contribute that until you can do more. The goal is to start and create a plan. Stop allowing the system to dictate your ability to invest in your future. You can do it. Creating small steps is the key.

Do you know anyone who gained wealth from their retirement account? The answer to this question is, NO! Retirees whom I know did not have enough money in their account to pay a year in living expenses. Yes, I know this sounds horrible but think about this; how many working-class families are truly investing or saving for their retirement? Many among the working-class people are employed just to pay their bills.

Many individuals were and are currently receiving social security and disability benefits to help meet their bills. How much money to do have left from your paycheck? With the money you have left over, you can try the Piggy Bank or Shoe Box challenge. If you are still saving your money under your bed mattress, you may be living in the Stone Age. Saving your money under a mattress is not a good idea. That thought needs to be removed from your mind.

By using a shoe box or piggy bank, you can start investing in the stock market will as little as $20-30 left over from your paycheck. If you have more money to save, then place more into the piggy bank. The goal of this challenge is to develop healthy saving habits. While you are completing this challenge, you can see how much money you are saving. Try placing $30 in a piggy bank or shoe box monthly. By the end of the year, you would have saved $360.00. Now that you have $360, you can begin to invest. If you decided not to invest once a year, establish a clear plan to invest every 3 to 6 months, etc. The goal is to make investing a good habit as well.

As you allow investing to become a healthy habit, you will see results in the future. This may not seem a lot to some people; however, for others, this approach is right down their lane. Let's say you, Investor Broke Jones, used $360.00 to purchase stock. Investor Broke Jones will be able to make the purchase. Investing in the stock market is what you make it. You can create your own financial goals that will best suit your life. How bad do you want to invest? Saving money is an excellent habit that we all can practice.

I believe small changes will help you on your money-saving journey. Time never slows down. It is up to us to seize every opportunity to turn our situation around. I am so grateful for the knowledge I have received lately to launch me into my destiny. Our negative financial habits don't disappear. It is up to us to work hard to establish plans and reevaluate our habits. I have created four tips how to save money below:

- We must get out of the habit of using our credit cards. Some of us have been in trouble with credit cards in the past (including myself). If you are tempted to use your credit card, you should leave them at home.

- Don't spend a lot of money entertaining your family. There many free activities in your local community. Realize that what your family wants most of all is your mind. Enjoy the park, backyard, or plant a garden.

- Cooking is another way to save money. I believe avoiding convenience food or fast food can be beneficial to your pockets. Instead of fast food, enjoy a home-cooked meal and pack your lunch for work.

- Make sure you cancel unused club memberships. For example, that gym membership you are not using. Just smile because everything will be alright. You can renew that membership at your convenience; however, if you are not properly using it, please cancel it.

Start with what you have. Your payday from the stock market begins when you start. You can sell or purchase stocks for as little $5-10 per trade. Don't make the mistake to believe you have to select the well-known companies to get paid from the stock market. Also, you do not need a stockbroker to invest your money for you. Using a stockbroker is for the Golden Ages. You know longer need to have a stockbroker like Bernie Madoff to invest your money for you.

If you can adequately understand the stock market and select companies that you can understand, I believe you can invest in the stock market on your own. With the proper training and education, who can invest your money better than you? I believe you guessed the answer which is, "NO ONE!" Now you can say out loud with confidence, "This is my money, and I can invest how I see fit." It is not a matter of picking the right stocks on a daily.

A way to get paid from the stock market is to invest in dividend stocks. A dividend stock will pay you quarterly income. Oh yeah! Yes, I like the sound of that! There are several dividend stocks that are listed on the stock exchanges which are 3M which pays around a 2.1% dividend yield; Abbott Laboratories, 1.9% dividend yield; Aflac, 2.2% dividend yield; Air Products, 2.4%; Archer Daniels Midland, 3.2% dividend yield; etc. Another way to make additional money is by compounding. This occurs when an investor reinvests their dividend income and plan to purchase more shares.

Lottery time:

As of November 2018, the Mega ball is 1.6 billion dollars. Many individuals are purchasing hundreds of tickets in hopes of winning the lottery. What would you do if you won the lottery? Believe it or not, winning the lottery appears to be the best strategy for some individuals. Winning the lottery can, in most cases, solve some, if not all your money problems. There is a show called "How the Lottery Changed My Life."

I believe winning the lottery comes with a hefty price. Do you believe money can buy you true happiness? It is clear the answer is, No. Just think about this, after you purchase everything you dreamed about during your childhood, as an adult, there is still a void. I believe winning the lottery can change your life but not in a good way. Most individuals who have won millions of dollars in the lottery, end up broke. These is due to their undisciplined spending habits. In some cases, individuals will go on extravagant spending sprees and vacations.

The odds of winning the lottery are slim to none. Did you know buying a ticket will increase your odds to win the lottery? Yes, this appears to be a redundant question. Based on the odds of winning, it is said that one is more likely to pass away on the way to get a ticket rather than win the lottery. A get rich quick scheme is not the way to go in life. There is only one way to the top, which is winning the lottery. I know winning the lottery seems to be something many people dream about. Please do not give up on your dream just yet. I will provide some tips for all the get rich quick dreamers.

It is more likely to be struck by lightning than to win the lottery. I do not know about you, but that sounds a bit harsh to me. Sadly, some individuals will win a lottery which can be the American dream to them. Without a financial plan, a person could easily spend their money very fast, however. Nevertheless, here is some excellent news. Winning the lottery is only one way to get rich quick.

If you are one of the few individuals who dream about becoming a millionaire, here are a few ways to help you do so. One way is to invest in the stock market in your early 20's. If you are in your 20's, you can develop an investing plan to become a millionaire by your 60's. If you are thinking anything like me, retiring in your 60's seems to be a long way off. You would instead enjoy what life had to offer you before age 60, right? To become a millionaire, which is a goal of mine as well, we need to develop several streams of income which I discussed earlier. Also, building your wealth portfolio by the asset classes I mentioned earlier is another way to generate streams of income.

If you are a lucky individual who wins the lottery, you will still need an investment strategy. An investment strategy is essential to keep your money for the long-term. A long-term investment plan will keep you from being one of the lottery winners on television who went from being a millionaire to being broke. The rules to success are based around creating the mindset to achieve greatness. Do you believe you can achieve financial freedom? Are you changing the way you think about money? Please keep the odds of winning the lottery in the back of your mind when heading to the store to purchase one. The tax on the poor is what the lottery is called. It was also said that most lottery ticket buyers are lower income individuals.

There is no single secret to success; however, there is a great reward when you can change your mindset, work effectively, and invest appropriately. I won the lottery when I changed the way I viewed my life and financial situation. Winning the lottery stems around your own personal belief in your ability to achieve greatness. Learn money matters in all your situation. Making your money properly has a direct relationship to investing the stock market. When a person has bills to pay along with other debts, they are less likely to invest in the stock market. In contrast to this, if you are debt free, the more money you have available to invest with.

Money management skills are essential when investing in the stock market. If you are wondering why then ask yourself this question. How can you invest in the stock market with no money? It is not possible. A person with negative financial habits may be less likely to think about saving or investing. Now let's talk about some of the money I have spent during my early adulthood. There were investment opportunities I could have taken advantage of had I known about investing. I know I would have. I reassured myself that my financial habits were not that bad; nevertheless, I patted myself on the back for spending crazy amounts of money and being thousands of dollars in debt.

You cannot justify negative financial habits. All negative habits must be properly adjusting when investing in the stock market. I like to say if you know better, you will do better. Now that you acknowledge a foundation of negative and positive financial habits, what are you going to do about it? Take a closer look at your inner circle. How many people in your inner circle invest in the stock market? Some individuals can feel as if they were born into the wrong family or are unlearned in financial accounting, but you must understand this is not an excuse for you to stop learning.

Do you realize some individuals stop learning after a certain age? We become accustomed to the norm and adapt to our environment. We become like a machine. We get up in the morning, go to work, come home, spend time with family or friends, go to bed, and repeat the pattern the next day. You should become a lifetime learner. You do not have to settle for what society is telling you about achieving your financial goals. All individuals were not created equally regarding their understanding of finances. Our financial habits can be a learned behavior. If so, what are you going to do about it? You are the only one who can change your financial situation.

The choice is yours. Start with smalls steps until you have reached your big goal. Think of achieving your goals like this: A short-term goal is two years or less. A medium goal is 2-4 years. A long-term is five years or more. You must establish a plan first to achieve one. What are your financial goals and how are you going to achieve them? You become the person you spend the most time with. The first step about the investing in the stock market is to change your mindset. You can invest in the stock market. You may be the first person in your family to learn about the stock market and invest in it. Guess what? So, am I. I came from a lower-class family. Some individuals in my family only had a retirement account, if that. So, you see, if I can do it, so can you. By the way, I am a busy single parent paving the way for my children. The cycle does not have to continue with you; it can stop with you.

The second step to investing in the stock market is to understand where you are financially. You will need to create a financial statement for your expenses. A financial statement is an overall report of all your expenses, income, liabilities, and assets. You will need to begin your financial statement with your income. How much money do you make a month? This will be your first line. If you have any extra income, include that income as well.

The second line is your expenses. On average, how much do you spend on food, shelter, clothing, transportation, pet items (toys or food), sports, entertainment, and personal maintenance (grooming)? I know you may have not enough room on the paper for all your expenses; however, this is needed so you can discover where you are financially.

In this section, you will be able to determine your spending habits. The third line is for your assets. An asset can be property, investment security, land, or something you will be able to draw cash from later. Assets are good to have. If you do not have any assets, please keep the third line blank. Do not beat yourself up about not having any assets. After learning about the stock market, you will have an insight into obtaining assets.

The fourth line is for your liabilities. A liability is debt. Make a list of your credit card, car loans, or any other debts you may have. Your network is your liabilities subtracted from your assets. Did you come up with a positive or negative number? The goal is not to owe more money than you have. Do you spend out more money than you have? If so, create a plan to generate more income. Create another list of items that you do very well. Are you able to be paid for your skill set?

An example would be if you can cut hair, tutor, or prepare taxes. Each of these things can be a potential avenue to generate more income. A sad reality to this exercise is that most of your spending will fall under certain lists. Try requesting a receipt every time you make a purchase. It does not matter if you are making a small or large purchase; make sure you get a receipt. This part is about accountability. Are you holding yourself accountable for your actions?

When it comes down to investing in the stock market when you are broke, you should create a plan to generate more income or create a budget. If you have an extra $20 a month, you have enough money to invest in the stock market. Good Times Restaurants Inc. is a stock that is available to purchase at $4.57 per share. You can at least purchase two of stocks in this company. How many shares you purchase in a company will depend upon the investment company.

Each investment company has trading fees to purchase a stock. Some trading fees differ in an amount based upon the company. Let's say you have an investment account with company ABC Investment Services. This company offers trading fees for $4.95. Now let's do some math. You can purchase three shares of Good Times Restaurants Inc. stocks for $4.57. Your trading fees will cost you $4.95. Customer Broke Jones purchased 3 x $4.57 = $13.71+4.95=$18.55. Now you have three shares of stock in Good Times Restaurants. The remaining money will sit in your account until you put more money in it.

You see, investing in the stock market is all about how you make it. I want you to know that three shares of stocks are far better than zero. The goal of generating wealth and receiving income comes from creating a plan. Real bosses create plans. If you fail to plan, then you plan to fail. How can you turn three shares to 300 or 3,000 shares? The answer is simple; create a plan. How often will you receive an extra $20.00? Will you receive an extra $20.00 weekly or biweekly?

Your lottery moment will come when you began to purchase companies you are already familiar with. It does not make any sense to purchase a company that makes dog sledding items if you are unfamiliar with that industry. Try to focus on companies you already spend your money with. Which type of car do you drive? Which type of gas do you put in your car? Do you play any sports? Do you take any prescription drugs or over-the-counter medicines? If so, what is the company that makes the drugs? You see, investing in the stock market is like peeling an apple. The outer layers represent the company that everyone can see and is very familiar with. The core represents the corporation that is behind the big name.

If your cell phone carrier is Verizon. It makes sense to invest your money in that company. Verizon Communications Inc. is traded on the New York Stock Exchange with the ticker symbol, VZ. Each company that is listed on the stock exchanges has a unique ticker symbol. The ticker symbol can have letters or numbers. As an investor, you will use a ticker symbol to place a trade. A share of Verizon's stock costs $56.81 as of October 2018. Verizon Communications is a dividend stock; therefore, you can receive dividend income on a quarterly basis.

VZ is one of the best networks in the U.S. Their company offers telephone, internet, and television packages as well as movie-streaming. Your chances of investing in a great company will depend on your knowledge of it. You should not invest in a company solely based upon, "This is my cell phone carrier." I suggest you invest in great companies that you have a proper understanding of. An investor will need to know what the company is about (industry), who the chief operators are (CEO), their competition, and have an understanding of their financial reports, etc.

The good news is that you should already have companies that you are passionate about or companies you already patronize. Nowadays, individuals want to run fast as they can to invest in the stock market without having a proper understanding of it. For your convivence, I offer mini and full investment courses for individuals just like you who are interested in learning more about the stock market. Be informed about your options for you may not want to purchase a laundry list of stocks that you spend your money on at this moment. You can enjoy investing in the stock market, but it is going to require some participation on your end. Creating an investment plan is essential whether purchases of stocks are short-term or long-term.

Another company to consider is Denbury Resources Inc. (DNR), which has shares listed at $6.05. This is a petroleum and natural gas company. With $20.00, you can purchase two shares of DNR stock for $12.10+$4.95=$17.05. Investing in the stock market comes down to companies you can make money from.

Take a small survey of companies that you like and already transact business with. If you already spend your money with them, why not receive a return on your investment? Whether you like Starbucks, McDonald's, Johnson & Johnson, Under Armor, or Exxon Mobile, take some time to discover how much the company's stock is worth. I believe you will be surprised. On a yearly basis, we spend tons of money on products; it is time to receive a return on our investments. I am going to say that and move on.

Nike, Inc. stock's price is $74.21 per share; however, individuals will spend most of their paycheck on a pair of shoes or garment for twice the price. After you purchase a pair of shoes every month or every other month, you should be able to purchase several shares of stocks per year. Now, let's do the math. Investor Broke Jones purchases a pair of Nike shoes six times in a year for $160.00 each. The total cost Investor Broke Jones will pay is $960.00.

Investor Broke Jones can purchase 11 shares in Nike, Inc.'s stock per year. Investor Broke Jones has purchased Nikes athletic shoes for the past ten years which totals $9,600. Just imagine the return on the investment if you purchased shares of stock in Nike or another company for the past ten years. Your main focus as an investor is to generate wealth and not continue to be a consumer.

Take the limits off:

I love to learn, and while investing in the stock market, I can do just that. I am uncomfortable. Yes, I am. Do I want to quit sometimes? Yes, I do! However, if I quit, what will happen to my children and others whom I am supposed to reach? Your financial freedom is so much bigger than you. It is time for you to take the limits off your mind. You can invest like a boss. You can generate wealth. You may start late in your life, but it is okay. It is better to start late than never to start investing. A person can take the limits off when it comes down to investing by letting go your emotions, diversifying your portfolio, educating yourself, and enhancing and changing your portfolio when needed. It is important for investors to remove their emotions when investing. The stock market fluctuates up and down throughout the day. Your emotions cannot match how the stock market is performing. Place your emotions in the back of your pocket and stick to your investment plan.

Diversification is important as well. Selecting a well-balanced portfolio allows you to retain different investment securities. I talk more about this in my other book *Stocks, Tips, and Stock Market Dips*. Education is the key when you are investing in the stock market. Like never before, an investor will need to research and educate themselves about investments they plan to buy.

Taking the limits off when you are investing in the stock market will require your participation and some level of risk. Take the limits off your mind to believe you can be successful. Would you prefer an investor to manage your money? Would you prefer to manage your portfolio on your own? You must decide how much time you have to learn about investing. There are several ways you can learn about investing in your spare time. The good news here is you do not need several hours to learn about the stock market. Start off learning about the stock market with 15 minutes per day. While you are learning about the stock market during the 15 minutes, make sure you are consistent and focused. The problem comes into play when you are trying to balance work, family, fitness, and social activities, etc. Remember, you decided to take the limits off and walk on this new journey to invest in the stock market. As I stated before, you will need to create a plan. While you are on this financial road to freedom, do not turn down free money.

Continue to add or match your 401(k) or other retirement plans. This will allow you to take advantage of free money that will grow until you retire. Always remember your 401(k) plan is an additional slice to the wealth pie. One of my main goals for financial freedom is a balance. There are no right or wrong investment strategies. The wrong investment strategies are the ones that you do not work on. Make sure you are treating your investment like a partnership. Check your emotions. Emotional investing will get you into some trouble. Taking the limits off will also require you to stop procrastinating from investing. Do you confuse your needs with your wants? Often, this is an example that delays individuals from investing. Before you have the thousands or millions of shares in a company, you will need to develop a plan to do so.

All investors try to avoid setbacks but heck, they come with the territory. This rule of thumb comes into play when you know what to cut, regroup, and refocus. Focus on financial freedom. As an investor, you will need to have a clear picture of the market and your goals. Understanding what you should cut is essential. The stock market will go up and down during the day, weeks, and months. Your main focus from investing in the stock market is not to lose money. You will have to know how many shares you should invest in a company. Your investor's plan should include an entrance and exit strategy.

Regrouping and refocusing examines your ability to address financial setbacks. A financial setback can feel similar to the wind getting knocked out of your chest. This will be a great timeframe to examine your overall portfolio. You will then be able to determine if you should sell or purchase stock. It does not matter if you are in love with a company, the company may not be a good investment.

Bringing balance and investing in the stock market will go hand and hand. Your investment strategy will change over time. The same will go for your risk level or perhaps you are just fine living in your current condition. You do not want to be a time waster. Reevaluate the times you have wasted. Are you on the road to financial freedom? In life, there are several situations that cause us to make a detour. It is sad to hear people agreeing to retire in their 60's. I have not met many who decided to retire at different ages. Being on the road to financial freedom allows your investments to create enough resources to cover your monthly income. If you are like me, you need more time for your hobbies, family, or vacation.

I know that the word *investing* will place fear into many people life. There are some individuals who are afraid or too confused to invest. An everyday tool you will need to help you to invest in the stock market is a newspaper. Today there are many investors who prefer to receive information about the stock market on the Internet. Yahoo Finance, Investopedia, Morningstar, *Barron's Magazine*, *The Wall Street Journal*, Motley Fool, MSN Money, or Seeking Alpha are all online stock market resources.

Try to think about investing in the stock market like building a house. Can you build your house on a sand foundation? In order to build a house, you will need a solid foundation. A contractor knows that you cannot build a house on a foundation full of sand. Can you imagine your dream home being built on a sand foundation? I believe you will be in for an unpleasant experience by doing that. Your beautiful home would most definitely float way when it rains.

A solid foundation will ensure your home will last for centuries. Think about the concept of building a home on a brick foundation when you are investing in the stock market. To be successful in the stock market, you will need to discover your risk level, financial goal, and investment strategies. Please remember that by purchasing a share in a company, you become part owner in that business.

Whenever you decide to invest in the stock market, you should determine your risk level. Some risk levels are conservative, moderate, and aggressive. After you determine your risk level, please examine your expectations. Make sure your expectations of investing in the stock market are obtainable. For example, some individuals are investing in the stock market to generate passive income. For others, you may want to invest in the stock market for long-term growth.

What should you place in your basket (investment portfolio)? Remember your investment "basket" will be unique. Stocks, bonds, or mutual funds can be included in your investment "basket portfolio." Your portfolio will not look like my portfolio and vice versa. In addition to this, you will need an investment strategy to invest in the stock market.

A great investor may want to include in their investment strategy who will manage it, types of investment securities, etc. For now, please relate investing in the stock market as a business decision. You are not investing in the stock market because it is the new thing to do. Spend 15 minutes each day to learn about the stock market. All investors will need to establish rules, goals, and investment strategies in order for them to succeed when investing in the stock market.

As mentioned earlier, there are several asset classes to generate wealth such as businesses, paper (investment securities such as stocks), commodities, and real estate. Investing in the stock market is considered a paper asset. Jeff Bezos, the founder of Amazon, took generated wealth to the next level. He started with a business which is one of the asset classes. Now, Amazon is available and has been for years as a stock. You can purchase Amazon if this company is a part of your investment strategy.

This giant e-commerce retailer has three sections to it which are North America, International, and Amazon Web Services. As of 2017, Amazon has a revenue of 43.7 billion dollars. What can you do with 1 billion dollars? We all would be millionaires if we invested 2,000 shares when Amazon first released its initial public offering (IPO).

Amazon Prime and Amazon Marketplace have made it convenient for individuals to shop at home. Amazon Prime allows shoppers to receive their purchases at home, business, or at a nearby Amazon Locker Service within two days. Amazon Marketplace allows shoppers to purchase items in an online shopping mall. There are many reasons to purchase Amazon, Inc.'s stocks and still be able to receive a high return on your investment.

I do not foresee Amazon's closing anytime soon. I believe Amazon is in it, to win it. Amazon has purchased Whole Foods' 2,000 grocery stores thus adding the grocery industry to their company's profile. I believe purchasing Whole Foods was a boss move! Consumers purchase their grocery items online and have them delivered to their home. UPS and FedEx must keep their eyes peeled because Amazon's next potential move is to establish their very own delivery service as discussed in 2018. Amazon, Inc. is a company to keep your eye on.

Dell Technology, Inc. is not a new company in town; however, investors have been receiving much buzz about it in the stock market news. I believe some investors may be excited about this news. Do you know Dell Technology, Inc. may be going public again after being private since 2013?

Dell Technology, Inc. has a revenue of 78.7 billion dollars. Dell Technology, Inc. may be a company to add to your watch list as well.

There are some stockbrokers, companies, and investors who make mistakes. I strongly recommend that you purchase stocks you are already familiar with and learn the inside and outside of the company. Take for example the story of Blockbuster Entertainment, Inc. which laughed the owner of Netflix out of their office. Blockbuster closed the remaining store in 2014 including all their distribution centers. Blockbuster, the once dominant video and game store, closed after a shift in the economy.

The cost of a Blockbuster rental was around $2.99 for a new release. An older release movie was $1.99. After the boom of Redbox, Blockbuster shortly closed the doors. Redbox and Netflix did not have extreme late fees for renting movies or games as Blockbuster. You see, moving and understanding market trends is essential when investing in the stock market. After the dramatic closing of thousands of Blockbuster stores, Blockbuster partnered with Dish. You could still make it a Blockbuster night and order a newly released movie in the comfort of your home. The company did not properly understand how the Internet was changing everything including movies. Blockbuster failing is a prime example for an investor to use. As an investor, creating an exit plan will save you from having a headache in the end.

Blockbuster was a company generating billions in income to $0. While Netflix went from $0 to billions. You see, being stuck in the past and bad management will cost you much money. If you begin to invest in a company that is failing, reevaluate your exit plan. You may want to sell your shares in the company before you lose all your money. Blockbuster failed because they decided not to adapt to the changing market, charging customer crazy amounts in late fees, and poor management. Investors can make millions buying wonderful companies. You can achieve financial freedom.

Payday:

The amount of money you need to invest in the stock market will depend on you. I know you hear of the phrase, "It takes money to make money!" This is true of any type of investing. How can you make money without having it? Some of the money you will have may come from your paycheck. Whether you are paid once, twice, or monthly, create a plan to fund your brokerage account with your paycheck. As a broke investor, you may wonder how much you need to start investing in the stock market.

There are two ways you can get started which are investing with a lump sum or dollar cost averaging. If you decide to invest with a lump sum, take into consideration your risk tolerance. Remember, you have the potential to make money, but you also run the risk of losing it. Additionally, you may take advantage of your money growing when you invest in a lump sum amount. If you decide on investing with a lump sum, try doing so with 40% of the total amount. This is a great way to evaluate the market to see if it is worth investing the rest of your money at a later point.

Dollar cost averaging (DCA) is a method used when investors minimize their risk by investing small amounts of money at a time. You can get in the habit of investing in the stock market by using this approach. When you use dollar cost averaging, you are purchasing one share or more at a fixed dollar amount and have a schedule to do so. Let's say you want to purchase Under Armour, Inc. for $19.72 per share. If you have $110.00 a month to invest with, you can purchase four shares per month. This is because you will need to include the brokerage commission fee for the trade. By using a dollar cost averaging approach, you can view the performance in stock every month if you choose to invest monthly.

Another example is having only $20.00 to invest in the stock market. Some stocks that are $20.00 and under are: Groupon (GRPN) at $4.50, NII Holding, Inc. (NIHD) at $5.17, or Oncolytics Biotech, Inc. (ONCY) at $2.22 per share. If you have $20.00 to invest, start with purchasing stocks once every three months. Even if you purchase four shares a year, it is better than purchasing no shares at all. Always include the online brokerage trade fees whether you are selling or purchasing investment securities. This fee will vary from company to company.

After you fund your account, it is essential to select the right stocks to meet your goals. An expensive stock does not necessarily mean it is a good investment just like a stock that is low in value is not considered to be a bad investment. When selecting a great company, be sure to analyze whether this is a great company. Think about their products, management, and financial reports which include earnings and revenue, valuation, accountability to shareholders, strengths, and weaknesses. Investing within one or several sectors are two options for you to investigate.

The stock market sectors are information technology, utilities, material, energy, industrials, health financials, telecom services, consumer discretionary, consumer staples, or industrials. Once you've decided on your goals, be sure to keep it simple. Choose quality stocks over quantity and evaluate your portfolio. Some online brokers to consider are: Robin Hood, Merrill Edge, Fidelity, Trade Station, Ally Invest, or Charles Schwab. Robin Hood is one online brokerage with no minimum deposit. Be sure to check the minimum amount you will need to open a brokerage account. Other things to consider when evaluating your brokerage account are customer service, tools, education, security, real-time quotes, updates, several investment products the company offers, maintenance fees, news, and accessibility.

After reading this book, you may still think that investing in the stock market is not for you. Frankly, you are not alone if you believe that by matching your retirement account, you will live a life of sipping iced tea while relaxing at the beach. I hate to be the bearer of terrible news, but the average person with a retirement account is not sipping iced tea on the beach; they are working at Walmart, Target, or the job they retired from on a part-time basis to meet the financial needs at home.

Think of wealth beyond your retirement accounts. Money invested in your retirement account will need to remain in the account until you are 59 ½ years old. The money invested in your retirement account is what I like to call addition to your wealth-building. If you want or need the money out of your account, you will be penalized for making an early withdrawal and taxes will be deducted. In terms of building wealth, you will need to build a wealth portfolio. Investing in stocks will represent an additional slice to your wealth pie or portfolio.

There are three tips I would like to leave with you on this investment journey. The first is to believe in yourself. Anything is possible when you believe. If you do not believe in yourself, who will? I believe you can change your financial lifestyle, however; it will come with a price. The price is determined by your ability to learn how to generate wealth and apply it. The next step is to change your mindset. A negative mindset about generating wealth will confine you to practicing unhealthy habits.

Whenever you decide to invest in the stock market, start with changing behaviors and impulsive vices that resulted in your financial bondage in the first place. Investing may seem like a dream to many people around the world because one main reason why people are not investing in the stock market is that they do not have any money. If you wait to start until you have a certain amount of money, you could be waiting for a very long time.

Now answer this question. How long have you waited to invest in the stock market? To invest in stocks, you need to adjust your lifestyle just like exercising or working at your job. I believe it is safe to say a person should make room in their budget to invest in stocks.

In the past, investing in stocks was not a part of my lifestyle because I did not believe it was for me. I did not have the money and I didn't understand it. Now that I teach individuals how to invest in the stock market, I made it apart of myself. You can start off doing simple things like reading the Wall Street Journal or books about the stock market. The time for making excuses are over. If you do not have the money to purchase a book for investing, visit your local library. I make sure to visit the library every week to learn and take advantage of free financial teachings offered at various locations. Other useful tools you can use to research your stocks are Yahoo Finance, CNBC, The Motley Fool, or Morningstar. Additionally, you can listen to webinars or podcasts to learn more information about the stock market. The time is now to invest, start with what you have.

The goal of investing in the stock market is to be ready. Don't wait until the stock market spirals downward; prepare yourself. Stay ready. An investor is always ready. For all the broke individuals reading this book, the stock market is a way to generate wealth. Make sure you increase your income, get out of debt, invest, and be consistent. Be positive, keep your emotions in your pocket, create a plan, and prepare. If you get off the road to financial freedom, try not to wait years to come back on it. With hard work and determination, you can invest in the stock market like a boss!

www.ingramcontent.com/pod-product-compliance
Lightning Source LLC
Chambersburg PA
CBHW031552210526
45464CB00003B/1267